WARM-UPS & ENERGY BOOSTERS

WARM-UPS & ENERGY BOOSTERS

Before jumping into scenes and characters, it's important to get everyone's bodies and minds ready to play. Warm-up games help children connect with each other, shake off shyness, and prepare for creative exploration. These activities are fast, simple, and full of laughter.

They are designed to:
- Build focus and confidence — helping players feel comfortable in the group.
- Boost energy and imagination — awakening both body and mind.
- Encourage teamwork — creating a sense of unity before diving into longer improvisations.

These games are perfect for the first 10–15 minutes of a session or anytime the group needs a burst of fun and focus. They mix movement, rhythm, and quick thinking — essential ingredients for any young improviser.

You can use them:
- At the start of class to energize and connect the group.
- Between activities as a playful break.
- At the end of a session to leave the group laughing and engaged.

Most of all, keep the spirit light. Mistakes are part of the fun — every giggle, clap, and silly move helps children grow their confidence and creativity.

ZIP ZAP ZOP

PLAYERS

6-20 PLAYERS

TIME

5-10 MINUTES

DESCRIPTION

A QUICK-PACED CIRCLE GAME WHERE PLAYERS PASS AN IMAGINARY "ENERGY ZAP" BY SAYING "ZIP", "ZAP", OR "ZOP".

OBJECTIVE

TO BOOST ENERGY, FOCUS ATTENTION, AND PRACTICE QUICK REACTIONS.

INSTRUCTIONS

1. PLAYERS STAND IN A CIRCLE.
2. THE FIRST PLAYER CLAPS THEIR HANDS, POINTS TO ANOTHER, AND SAYS "ZIP."
3. THE NEXT PLAYER PASSES IT ON BY SAYING "ZAP."
4. THE FOLLOWING PASSES IT WITH "ZOP."
5. THE CYCLE REPEATS: ZIP → ZAP → ZOP → ZIP...

VARIATIONS

- REVERSE THE ORDER (ZOP → ZAP → ZIP).
- ADD MOVEMENTS WITH EACH WORD.
- SPEED IT UP!

NAME AND MOVEMENT

PLAYERS

6-25 PLAYERS

TIME

10-15 MINUTES

DESCRIPTION

A SIMPLE INTRODUCTION GAME WHERE EACH PLAYER SAYS THEIR NAME AND ADDS A UNIQUE MOVEMENT OR GESTURE. THE GROUP REPEATS THE NAME AND MOVEMENT TOGETHER

OBJECTIVE

TO HELP THE GROUP LEARN NAMES, BUILD CONFIDENCE, AND ENCOURAGE SELF-EXPRESSION.

INSTRUCTIONS

1. PLAYERS STAND IN A CIRCLE.
2. THE FIRST PLAYER SAYS: "MY NAME IS [NAME]" AND ADDS A MOVEMENT OR GESTURE (E.G., JUMP, CLAP, WAVE).
3. THE GROUP REPEATS THE NAME AND THE MOVEMENT TOGETHER.
4. CONTINUE AROUND THE CIRCLE UNTIL EVERYONE HAS GONE.
5. OPTION: AT THE END, TRY TO GO AROUND THE CIRCLE REPEATING ALL NAMES AND MOVEMENTS IN ORDER.

VARIATIONS

- ADD A SOUND WITH THE MOVEMENT.
- PLAY "FAST ROUND": NO REPEATING, JUST QUICK INTRODUCTIONS.
- TRY BACKWARDS ORDER (LAST PLAYER INTRODUCES, GROUP REPEATS).

THE MIRROR

PLAYERS

PAIRS (WHOLE GROUP WORKS IN PAIRS)

TIME

5-10 MINUTES

DESCRIPTION

TWO PLAYERS FACE EACH OTHER; ONE LEADS SLOW MOVEMENTS WHILE THE OTHER COPIES EXACTLY LIKE A MIRROR.

OBJECTIVE

DEVELOP FOCUS, OBSERVATION, AND TEAMWORK.

INSTRUCTIONS

1. FORM PAIRS FACING EACH OTHER.
2. ONE IS THE LEADER, THE OTHER THE MIRROR.
3. LEADER MOVES SLOWLY; MIRROR COPIES EXACTLY.
4. AFTER 1-2 MINUTES, SWITCH ROLES.

VARIATIONS

- TRY FAST MOVEMENTS.
- BOTH LEAD AT THE SAME TIME.
- ADD EMOTIONS (ANGRY, HAPPY, SLEEPY).

PASS THE CLAP

PLAYERS

6-20 PLAYERS

TIME

5-10 MINUTES

DESCRIPTION

PLAYERS STAND IN A CIRCLE AND PASS A CLAP AROUND BY MAKING EYE CONTACT, CLAPPING AT THE SAME TIME, AND SENDING IT TO THE NEXT PLAYER. THE GOAL IS TO KEEP THE RHYTHM FLOWING.

OBJECTIVE

TO BUILD FOCUS, RHYTHM, TEAMWORK, AND GROUP AWARENESS.

INSTRUCTIONS

1. PLAYERS STAND IN A CIRCLE.
2. ONE PLAYER MAKES EYE CONTACT WITH A NEIGHBOR AND BOTH CLAP AT THE SAME TIME.
3. THAT NEIGHBOR THEN TURNS TO THE NEXT PLAYER, MAKES EYE CONTACT, AND CLAPS TOGETHER.
4. THE "CLAP" CONTINUES AROUND THE CIRCLE.
5. ONCE THE GROUP GETS THE RHYTHM, TRY TO SPEED IT UP.

VARIATIONS

- REVERSE DIRECTION AT ANY TIME.
- PASS TWO CLAPS AROUND THE CIRCLE AT THE SAME TIME.
- TRY SENDING THE CLAP ACROSS THE CIRCLE WITH EYE CONTACT.

ENERGY BALL

PLAYERS

6-20 PLAYERS

TIME

10 MINUTES

DESCRIPTION

PLAYERS IMAGINE HOLDING AN "ENERGY BALL." THEY PASS IT AROUND THE CIRCLE WITH A SOUND AND MOVEMENT, CHANGING ITS SIZE, WEIGHT, OR ENERGY EACH TIME.

OBJECTIVE

TO ENCOURAGE IMAGINATION, BODY EXPRESSION, AND GROUP CONNECTION.

INSTRUCTIONS

1. PLAYERS STAND IN A CIRCLE.
2. ONE PLAYER MIMES HOLDING A BALL AND ADDS A SOUND.
3. THEY "THROW" IT TO ANOTHER PLAYER.
4. THE NEXT PLAYER CATCHES IT AND CAN CHANGE ITS SIZE, WEIGHT, OR ENERGY (TINY, HUGE, HEAVY, BOUNCY, STICKY, ETC.).
5. CONTINUE PASSING IT UNTIL EVERYONE HAS TRANSFORMED THE BALL.

VARIATIONS

- PASS TWO ENERGY BALLS AT ONCE.
- CHANGE INTO DIFFERENT OBJECTS.
- ADD EMOTIONS TO THE BALL (ANGRY BALL, HAPPY BALL, SLEEPY BALL).

SOUND MACHINE

PLAYERS

6-30 PLAYERS

TIME

10-15 MINUTES

DESCRIPTION

PLAYERS CREATE A COLLECTIVE "MACHINE" BY ADDING REPETITIVE SOUNDS AND MOVEMENTS ONE BY ONE, UNTIL THE GROUP FORMS A LIVING SOUND MACHINE.

OBJECTIVE

TO BUILD GROUP AWARENESS, RHYTHM, AND CREATIVITY.

INSTRUCTIONS

1. PLAYERS STAND IN A CIRCLE.
2. ONE PLAYER STARTS WITH A REPETITIVE SOUND AND A MOVEMENT (E.G., "CH-CH" WHILE MOVING ARMS).
3. THE NEXT ADDS A NEW SOUND AND MOVEMENT, THEN ANOTHER PLAYER ADDS THEIRS.
4. CONTINUE UNTIL THE WHOLE GROUP IS PART OF THE MACHINE.
5. THE FACILITATOR CAN "CONDUCT" THE MACHINE: LOUDER, SOFTER, FASTER, SLOWER, STOP.

VARIATIONS

- DIVIDE INTO TWO "MACHINES" THAT INTERACT.
- ADD AN EMOTION TO THE MACHINE (HAPPY, SCARY, SLEEPY).
- CREATE A "BROKEN MACHINE" WHERE PARTS GO WRONG.

FOCUS & LISTENING GAMES

FOCUS & LISTENING GAMES

Improvisation isn't just about speaking — it's about listening, observing, and responding. These Focus & Listening Games train young players to pay attention to their partners, react in the moment, and stay fully present on stage.

In these activities, children practice:

- Active listening — tuning in to others' words, sounds, and movements.
- Concentration — staying alert even when things get silly or unexpected.
- Quick response — building the habit of saying "yes" to ideas and acting on them.

The goal is to strengthen group awareness and help players work as an ensemble — a team that thinks and moves together. Through rhythm, eye contact, and observation, children discover that great scenes grow from truly listening, not just talking.

These games are perfect for moments when the group needs to refocus, calm down, or connect after high-energy activities. They balance excitement with attention, teaching young improvisers that silence, patience, and timing can be just as powerful as laughter and movement.

Encourage players to notice everything — a gesture, a sound, a tiny idea — because in improvisation, the smallest detail can inspire the biggest story.

WORD-AT-A-TIME STORY

PLAYERS

4-15 PLAYERS

TIME

10-15 MINUTES

DESCRIPTION

PLAYERS CREATE A STORY TOGETHER BY ADDING ONE WORD AT A TIME IN SEQUENCE.

OBJECTIVE

O PRACTICE LISTENING CAREFULLY, BUILDING ON OTHERS' IDEAS, AND STORYTELLING.

INSTRUCTIONS

1. PLAYERS SIT OR STAND IN A CIRCLE.
2. ONE PLAYER STARTS WITH A SINGLE WORD.
3. THE NEXT ADDS ONE WORD, THEN THE NEXT, AND SO ON, BUILDING A SENTENCE.
4. CONTINUE UNTIL THE STORY NATURALLY ENDS.

VARIATIONS

- PLAY WITH TWO WORDS AT A TIME.
- ADD A THEME (SPACE, JUNGLE, SCHOOL).
- CREATE A "SILLY STORY" RULE (EVERY SENTENCE MUST INCLUDE A BANANA).

ONE-WORD-AT-A-TIME DRAWING

PLAYERS

4-15 PLAYERS

TIME

8-10 MINUTES

DESCRIPTION

PLAYERS "DRAW" IN THE AIR TOGETHER, ONE LINE AT A TIME, BY DESCRIBING OR MIMING THE DRAWING. THE GROUP BUILDS ONE PICTURE COLLECTIVELY.

OBJECTIVE

TO TRAIN IMAGINATION, COOPERATION, AND NON-VERBAL COMMUNICATION.

INSTRUCTIONS

1. PLAYERS STAND FACING THE GROUP.
2. ONE PLAYER STARTS "DRAWING" AN OBJECT IN THE AIR WITH THEIR FINGER.
3. THE NEXT CONTINUES THE DRAWING BY ADDING DETAILS.
4. CONTINUE UNTIL THE GROUP AGREES THE DRAWING IS FINISHED.

VARIATIONS

- ADD SOUND EFFECTS.
- DRAW A CHARACTER INSTEAD OF AN OBJECT.
- TURN THE DRAWING INTO A SHORT SCENE.

NUMBER COUNT

PLAYERS

6-20 PLAYERS

TIME

5-10 MINUTES

DESCRIPTION

THE GROUP TRIES TO COUNT ALOUD FROM 1 TO 20, BUT ONLY ONE PERSON CAN SPEAK AT A TIME, AND IF TWO SPEAK TOGETHER, THE COUNT STARTS OVER.

OBJECTIVE

TO BUILD PATIENCE, FOCUS, AND GROUP AWARENESS.

INSTRUCTIONS

1. PLAYERS SIT IN A CIRCLE.
2. AS A GROUP, TRY TO COUNT TO 20 (OR ANOTHER TARGET NUMBER).
3. ANY PLAYER MAY SAY THE NEXT NUMBER, BUT ONLY ONE AT A TIME.
4. IF TWO OR MORE SPEAK TOGETHER, RESTART FROM 1.

VARIATIONS

- COUNT BACKWARDS FROM 20 TO 1.
- REPLACE NUMBERS WITH SOUNDS OR CLAPS.
- TRY REACHING A HIGHER TARGET (30 OR 50).

COPY CIRCLE

PLAYERS

6-20 PLAYERS

TIME

10-15 MINUTES

DESCRIPTION

A MOVEMENT GAME WHERE PLAYERS STAND IN A CIRCLE AND COPY EACH OTHER'S MOVEMENTS IN SEQUENCE, CREATING A FLOW OF IMITATION.

OBJECTIVE

TO TRAIN OBSERVATION, MEMORY, AND GROUP SYNCHRONIZATION.

INSTRUCTIONS

1. PLAYERS STAND IN A CIRCLE.
2. ONE PLAYER MAKES A SIMPLE MOVEMENT (E.G., CLAP, SPIN, STRETCH).
3. THE NEXT PLAYER REPEATS IT, THEN ADDS A NEW MOVEMENT.
4. THE THIRD COPIES THE TWO MOVEMENTS, THEN ADDS A THIRD.
5. CONTINUE UNTIL EVERYONE HAS CONTRIBUTED.

VARIATIONS

- PLAY WITHOUT SPEAKING.
- TRY TO GO FASTER AND FASTER.
- AT THE END, PERFORM THE ENTIRE SEQUENCE TOGETHER.

GIBBERISH CONVERSATIONS

PLAYERS

PAIRS OR SMALL GROUPS

TIME

10 MINUTES

DESCRIPTION

PLAYERS TALK TO EACH OTHER USING ONLY NONSENSE SOUNDS ("GIBBERISH") INSTEAD OF REAL WORDS.

OBJECTIVE

TO FOCUS ON TONE, BODY LANGUAGE, AND EMOTIONAL EXPRESSION BEYOND WORDS.

INSTRUCTIONS

1. DIVIDE PLAYERS INTO PAIRS.
2. THEY "TALK" TO EACH OTHER IN GIBBERISH FOR 1-2 MINUTES.
3. ENCOURAGE EXPRESSIVE TONE, GESTURES, AND EMOTIONS.
4. OPTION: HAVE PAIRS PERFORM THEIR GIBBERISH CONVERSATIONS FOR THE GROUP.

VARIATIONS

- GIVE THEM A SITUATION (ORDERING FOOD, ARGUING, ASKING DIRECTIONS).
- PLAY IN GROUPS OF THREE.
- ADD A "TRANSLATOR" WHO EXPLAINS IN REAL WORDS WHAT THEY "SAID."

CREATIVITY & STORYTELLING

CREATIVITY & STORYTELLING

Every great improviser is, at heart, a storyteller. In this section, players learn how to use their imagination to build stories together — creating characters, adventures, and worlds from nothing but ideas, sounds, and movement.

These games encourage children to:

- Invent freely — saying "yes, and..." to new possibilities.
- Collaborate — building on each other's ideas instead of competing.
- Find structure — understanding beginnings, middles, and endings in playful ways.

Each activity invites players to think creatively while having fun, transforming ordinary moments into extraordinary tales. The focus is on imagination, cooperation, and joy, not perfection. Mistakes become new story twists, and laughter becomes part of the plot.

These games can be used to:

- Spark creative thinking before scene work.
- Help players learn how stories are built.
- Encourage confidence in speaking and sharing ideas.

In the world of improvisation, there are no scripts and no wrong answers — only bold choices, teamwork, and endless creativity. With these storytelling games, every child becomes both an author and an actor, shaping stories that only they could imagine.

THE ALPHABET GAME

PLAYERS

2-6 PLAYERES

TIME

10-15 MINUTES

DESCRIPTION

PLAYERS CREATE A SCENE OR DIALOGUE WHERE EACH SENTENCE BEGINS WITH THE NEXT LETTER OF THE ALPHABET.

OBJECTIVE

TO DEVELOP CREATIVITY, VOCABULARY, AND QUICK THINKING.

INSTRUCTIONS

1. TWO PLAYERS START A SCENE.
2. THE FIRST LINE BEGINS WITH "A," THE NEXT WITH "B," THEN "C," AND SO ON.
3. CONTINUE UNTIL REACHING "Z" (OR UNTIL THE SCENE ENDS NATURALLY).

VARIATIONS

- PLAY ONLY FROM A TO M FOR YOUNGER KIDS.
- ALLOW SKIPPING LETTERS IF STUCK.
- DO IT IN SPANISH AND THEN IN ENGLISH

FORTUNATELY-UNFORTUNATELY

PLAYERS

4-12 PLAYERS

TIME

10-15 MINUTES

DESCRIPTION

PLAYERS TELL A STORY ALTERNATING BETWEEN FORTUNATE AND UNFORTUNATE EVENTS.

OBJECTIVE

TO TRAIN STORYTELLING, HUMOR, AND FLEXIBILITY.

INSTRUCTIONS

1. PLAYERS SIT IN A CIRCLE.
2. THE FIRST PLAYER STARTS: "FORTUNATELY..." AND ADDS AN EVENT.
3. THE NEXT CONTINUES WITH "UNFORTUNATELY..."
4. ALTERNATE UNTIL THE STORY ENDS.

VARIATIONS

- SWITCH TO "HAPPILY-SADLY."
- DO IT IN PAIRS AS A DIALOGUE.
- ADD A THEME (SCHOOL, SPACE, JUNGLE).

STORY CUBES (WITH DICE OR CARDS)

PLAYERS

2-10 PLAYERS

TIME

10-15 MINUTES

DESCRIPTION

PLAYERS USE DICE OR CARDS WITH IMAGES TO INSPIRE A COLLECTIVE STORY.

OBJECTIVE

TO SPARK CREATIVITY AND COLLABORATIVE STORYTELLING.

INSTRUCTIONS

1. ROLL DICE (WITH PICTURES) OR PICK CARDS.
2. PLAYERS TAKE TURNS ADDING PARTS OF THE STORY INSPIRED BY THE IMAGES.
3. CONTINUE UNTIL ALL IMAGES ARE USED IN THE STORY.

VARIATIONS

- USE DRAWINGS MADE BY THE KIDS.
- CREATE A "GENRE" (FAIRY TALE, SCI-FI, MYSTERY).
- PLAY IN PAIRS AND SHARE STORIES WITH THE GROUP.

FAIRY TALE REMIX

PLAYERS

4-10 PLAYERS

TIME

15-20 MINUTES

DESCRIPTION

PLAYERS TAKE A FAMILIAR FAIRY TALE AND RETELL IT WITH A SILLY TWIST, NEW ENDING, OR IN A DIFFERENT STYLE.

OBJECTIVE

TO EXPLORE CREATIVITY, PARODY, AND COLLECTIVE STORYTELLING.

INSTRUCTIONS

1. PICK A WELL-KNOWN FAIRY TALE (LITTLE RED RIDING HOOD, THREE LITTLE PIGS).
2. RETELL THE STORY AS A GROUP.
3. ADD TWISTS: CHANGE CHARACTERS, SETTING, OR THE ENDING.
4. PERFORM THE NEW VERSION FOR EVERYONE.

VARIATIONS

- TELL IT AS A SCI-FI STORY.
- USE ANIMALS OR SUPERHEROES INSTEAD OF THE ORIGINAL CHARACTERS.
- CHANGE THE ENDING COMPLETELY.

BUILD A STORY CHAIN

PLAYERS

5-15 PLAYERS

TIME

10 MINUTES

DESCRIPTION

A COLLABORATIVE STORYTELLING ACTIVITY WHERE EACH PLAYER ADDS ONE SENTENCE TO CONTINUE THE STORY.

OBJECTIVE

TO BUILD TEAMWORK, IMAGINATION, AND SEQUENTIAL THINKING.

INSTRUCTIONS

1. PLAYERS SIT IN A CIRCLE.
2. ONE PLAYER STARTS A STORY WITH A SENTENCE.
3. EACH PERSON ADDS ONE NEW SENTENCE IN TURN.
4. CONTINUE UNTIL THE STORY FEELS COMPLETE.

VARIATIONS

- ADD A THEME (A LOST TREASURE, A HAUNTED HOUSE).
- LIMIT SENTENCES TO 5 WORDS.
- CREATE TWO STORIES IN PARALLEL.

WHAT HAPPENS NEXT?

PLAYERS

6-20 PLAYERS

TIME

10-15 MINUTES

DESCRIPTION

PLAYERS TELL A STORY TOGETHER, BUT AT KEY MOMENTS THE GROUP OR AUDIENCE DECIDES "WHAT HAPPENS NEXT?" AND THE STORYTELLER MUST CONTINUE WITH THE SUGGESTION.

OBJECTIVE

TO DEVELOP ADAPTABILITY, CREATIVITY, AND GROUP PARTICIPATION IN STORYTELLING.

INSTRUCTIONS

1. ONE OR TWO PLAYERS BEGIN TELLING OR ACTING OUT A STORY.
2. AT ANY POINT, THE FACILITATOR OR AUDIENCE SAYS: "WHAT HAPPENS NEXT?"
3. THE PLAYERS MUST INSTANTLY CONTINUE WITH A NEW TWIST OR IDEA.
4. CONTINUE UNTIL THE STORY HAS A FUN OR SURPRISING ENDING.

VARIATIONS

- AUDIENCE SUGGESTS A GENRE (HORROR, COMEDY, FANTASY).
- MULTIPLE PLAYERS TAG IN TO CONTINUE THE STORY.
- USE A RANDOM OBJECT AS INSPIRATION.

MOVEMENT & SPACE

MOVEMENT & SPACE

Improvisation lives not only in words, but in the body. These games help children discover how to use movement, posture, and space to express emotions, tell stories, and connect with others — without needing to speak at all.

Through movement-based play, children learn to:

- Become aware of their bodies — how they move, balance, and take up space.
- Express emotions physically — showing feelings through gestures and rhythm.
- Use the stage or classroom creatively — exploring distance, direction, and focus.

These activities combine energy, coordination, and imagination. Players might move like animals, explore invisible worlds, or transform their bodies into objects or elements of nature. Every motion becomes a tool for storytelling.

They are especially useful when:

- The group has extra energy to release.
- You want to wake up creativity through physical play.
- You're introducing the idea that actions can speak louder than words.

Encourage students to move boldly, make big choices, and respect each other's personal space. In these games, movement becomes a language — one that every child can speak fluently.

HUMAN MACHINE

PLAYERS
6-20 PLAYERS

TIME
10-15 MINUTES

DESCRIPTION
PLAYERS BUILD AN IMAGINARY MACHINE BY ADDING MOVEMENTS AND SOUNDS, ONE AT A TIME, UNTIL THE WHOLE GROUP IS PART OF IT.

OBJECTIVE
TO PRACTICE GROUP CREATIVITY, RHYTHM, AND TEAMWORK.

INSTRUCTIONS
1. ONE PLAYER STEPS FORWARD AND STARTS A REPETITIVE SOUND AND MOVEMENT.
2. ANOTHER JOINS WITH A NEW SOUND AND MOVEMENT THAT FITS.
3. EACH PLAYER ADDS SOMETHING UNTIL A "MACHINE" IS CREATED.
4. LET THE MACHINE RUN FOR A WHILE, THEN STOP.

VARIATIONS
- BUILD MACHINES WITH A THEME (WASHING MACHINE, TIME MACHINE, SPACESHIP).
- CHANGE SPEED GRADUALLY (SLOW, THEN FASTER).
- PERFORM THE MACHINE IN SILENCE (ONLY MOVEMENTS).

STATUES (FREEZE & TRANSFORM)

PLAYERS

6-20 PLAYERS

TIME

10 MINUTES

DESCRIPTION

A CLASSIC STILLNESS GAME WHERE PLAYERS FREEZE AS STATUES IN DIFFERENT POSES.

OBJECTIVE

TO PRACTICE BODY EXPRESSION, STILLNESS, AND IMAGINATION.

INSTRUCTIONS

1. PLAYERS MOVE AROUND THE SPACE.
2. WHEN THE FACILITATOR CALLS "STATUE!", THEY FREEZE IN A POSE.
3. EACH TIME, CHOOSE A THEME (ANIMAL, SUPERHERO, MONSTER, DANCER).
4. CONTINUE WITH NEW STATUES.

VARIATIONS

- HAVE PLAYERS HOLD THEIR STATUE WHILE OTHERS WALK AROUND AND OBSERVE.
- CREATE STATUES IN PAIRS OR GROUPS OF THREE.
- TURN STATUES INTO A SHORT SCENE.

'FREEZE & MELT

PLAYERS

5 -20 PLAYERS

TIME

10 MINUTES

DESCRIPTION

PLAYERS MOVE FREELY AROUND THE SPACE. WHEN THE FACILITATOR CALLS "FREEZE!" THEY STOP INSTANTLY. ON "MELT!" THEY SLOWLY MOVE AGAIN.

OBJECTIVE

TO IMPROVE BODY CONTROL, AWARENESS, AND LISTENING.

INSTRUCTIONS

1. PLAYERS SPREAD OUT IN THE SPACE.
2. THEY MOVE AROUND IN ANY WAY THEY LIKE.
3. WHEN THE FACILITATOR SAYS "FREEZE!", EVERYONE MUST STOP IMMEDIATELY.
4. ON "MELT!", PLAYERS MOVE AGAIN, SLOWLY AT FIRST, THEN NORMALLY.

VARIATIONS

- ADD EMOTIONS (FREEZE LIKE YOU'RE SCARED, MELT LIKE YOU'RE HAPPY).
- PLAY WITH MUSIC (FREEZE WHEN THE MUSIC STOPS).
- INTRODUCE DIFFERENT COMMANDS ("FLY!", "SHRINK!", "GROW!").

MIRROR GAME

PLAYERS

PAIRS

TIME

10 MINUTES

DESCRIPTION

PLAYERS WORK IN PAIRS, ONE LEADING AND THE OTHER MIRRORING THEIR MOVEMENTS AS IF THEY WERE A REFLECTION.

OBJECTIVE

TO DEVELOP CONCENTRATION, NON-VERBAL COMMUNICATION, AND PHYSICAL COORDINATION.

INSTRUCTIONS

1. PLAYERS FORM PAIRS AND FACE EACH OTHER.
2. ONE PLAYER MOVES SLOWLY WHILE THE OTHER COPIES AS IF IN A MIRROR.
3. SWITCH ROLES AFTER 1-2 MINUTES.
4. TRY MOVEMENTS WITH DIFFERENT SPEEDS AND LEVELS.

VARIATIONS

- DO IT WITHOUT DESIGNATING A LEADER—BOTH TRY TO MOVE TOGETHER.
- ADD MUSIC FOR INSPIRATION.
- TRY WITH FACIAL EXPRESSIONS ONLY.

WALK LIKE...

PLAYERS

6 - 20 PLAYERS

TIME

10 MINUTES

DESCRIPTION

PLAYERS EXPLORE THE SPACE WALKING IN DIFFERENT STYLES (ANIMALS, EMOTIONS, CHARACTERS).

OBJECTIVE

TO FREE PHYSICAL EXPRESSION AND CONNECT IMAGINATION WITH MOVEMENT.

INSTRUCTIONS

1. PLAYERS WALK AROUND THE SPACE.
2. THE FACILITATOR CALLS OUT "WALK LIKE A LION!" OR "WALK LIKE YOU'RE VERY TIRED!"
3. PLAYERS IMMEDIATELY CHANGE THEIR WALK TO MATCH THE SUGGESTION.
4. CONTINUE WITH NEW PROMPTS.

VARIATIONS

- PLAYERS CAN GIVE PROMPTS INSTEAD OF THE FACILITATOR.
- WALK WITH MUSIC OF DIFFERENT MOODS.
- COMBINE TWO PROMPTS ("WALK LIKE A ROBOT WHO IS SAD").

OBJECT TRANSFORMATION

PLAYERS

6-15 PLAYERS

TIME

10 MINUTES

DESCRIPTION

A SIMPLE OBJECT IS PASSED AROUND, AND EACH PLAYER PRETENDS IT IS SOMETHING COMPLETELY DIFFERENT.

OBJECTIVE

TO BOOST IMAGINATION, CREATIVITY, AND FLEXIBLE THINKING.

INSTRUCTIONS

1. CHOOSE A SIMPLE OBJECT (STICK, BALL, SCARF).
2. THE FIRST PLAYER MIMES USING IT AS SOMETHING NEW (A SWORD, MICROPHONE, FISHING ROD).
3. AFTER A FEW SECONDS, PASS IT TO THE NEXT PLAYER.
4. CONTINUE UNTIL EVERYONE HAS TRANSFORMED THE OBJECT.

VARIATIONS

- PLAYERS MUST USE SOUND EFFECTS TOO.
- TRANSFORM THE OBJECT INTO EMOTIONS (SAD UMBRELLA, ANGRY CHAIR).
- PASS TWO OBJECTS AT THE SAME TIME.

SLOW MOTION OLYMPICS

PLAYERS

6-20 PLAYERS

TIME

10-15 MINUTES

DESCRIPTION

PLAYERS COMPETE IN IMAGINARY OLYMPIC EVENTS, BUT EVERYTHING HAPPENS IN SLOW MOTION.

OBJECTIVE

TO PRACTICE PHYSICAL EXPRESSION, TIMING, AND GROUP FUN.

INSTRUCTIONS

1. THE FACILITATOR ANNOUNCES AN OLYMPIC SPORT (RUNNING, SWIMMING, WRESTLING).
2. PLAYERS ACT OUT THE EVENT IN EXAGGERATED SLOW MOTION.
3. OTHERS CHEER AS THE "AUDIENCE."
4. ROTATE PLAYERS SO EVERYONE COMPETES.

VARIATIONS

- ADD SILLY SPORTS (TOOTHBRUSHING, SANDWICH-MAKING).
- USE INSTANT REPLAYS.
- DO IT IN "FAST FORWARD" INSTEAD OF SLOW MOTION.

ANIMALS AT THE ZOO

PLAYERS

6-20 PLAYERS

TIME

10 MINUTES

DESCRIPTION

PLAYERS ACT AS DIFFERENT ANIMALS IN A ZOO, SHOWING HOW THEY MOVE, SOUND, AND INTERACT.

OBJECTIVE

TO EXPLORE PHYSICALITY, IMAGINATION, AND GROUP PLAY.

INSTRUCTIONS

1. PLAYERS CHOOSE OR ARE ASSIGNED ANIMALS.
2. EACH PLAYER ACTS LIKE THEIR ANIMAL IN THE "ZOO."
3. THE FACILITATOR (ZOOKEEPER) INTRODUCES OR DIRECTS THEM.
4. ANIMALS MAY INTERACT—BE PLAYFUL BUT SAFE.

VARIATIONS

- FREEZE WHEN THE ZOOKEEPER COMES.
- DO IT IN SLOW MOTION.
- GUESS THE ANIMALS WITHOUT TELLING NAMES.

MOVEMENT & SPACE

"SPACE WALK

PLAYERS
6-20 PLAYERS

TIME
10 MINUTES

DESCRIPTION
PLAYERS IMAGINE WALKING IN SPACE, DEALING WITH GRAVITY, FLOATING, AND EXPLORING PLANETS.

OBJECTIVE
TO PRACTICE IMAGINATION, BODY CONTROL, AND TEAMWORK.

INSTRUCTIONS
1. PLAYERS MOVE AS ASTRONAUTS WITH HEAVY SPACE SUITS.
2. TRY FLOATING, JUMPING IN SLOW MOTION, OR AVOIDING ASTEROIDS.
3. THE FACILITATOR CAN ADD EVENTS: "LOW GRAVITY," "METEOR SHOWER," "ALIEN ENCOUNTER."

VARIATIONS
- USE MUSIC TO SET THE SPACE ATMOSPHERE.
- PLAYERS EXPLORE DIFFERENT PLANETS WITH UNIQUE CONDITIONS.
- ADD SOUND EFFECTS (BREATHING, RADIO STATIC).

CHARACTERS & EMOTIONS

CHARACTERS & EMOTIONS

Improvisation comes to life through the people we become on stage. These games invite children to explore different characters, feelings, and points of view, helping them step into someone else's shoes with imagination and empathy.

In this section, players learn to:

- Create distinct characters using voice, movement, and attitude.
- Express emotions clearly — from joy and excitement to fear, sadness, or surprise.
- Understand how emotions drive stories and relationships in a scene.

By experimenting with personalities and feelings, children gain confidence and emotional awareness. They discover that there's no single "right way" to act — every choice adds color and depth to the story.

These activities can be playful, funny, or even tender. A character might be a grumpy dragon, a nervous detective, or a cheerful robot — anything the imagination allows!
Use these games when you want to:

- Encourage creativity and self-expression.
- Help players connect emotionally with their characters.
- Build empathy and teamwork through shared storytelling.

Remind your group: every character has a heart. Even the silliest ones have something to say — and in improvisation, every feeling is welcome.

EMOTION SWITCH

PLAYERS

4-12 PLAYERS

TIME

10 MINUTES

DESCRIPTION

PLAYERS ACT OUT A SIMPLE SCENE BUT MUST SWITCH EMOTIONS WHENEVER THE LEADER CALLS OUT A NEW ONE.

OBJECTIVE

TO PRACTICE FLEXIBILITY, EMOTIONAL EXPRESSION, AND QUICK REACTIONS.

INSTRUCTIONS

1. TWO OR MORE PLAYERS START A SIMPLE SCENE (BUYING ICE CREAM, WAITING FOR A BUS).
2. THE FACILITATOR CALLS OUT AN EMOTION (ANGRY, EXCITED, SAD).
3. THE PLAYERS CONTINUE THE SAME SCENE BUT WITH THE NEW EMOTION.
4. KEEP SWITCHING EMOTIONS AS THE GAME CONTINUES.

VARIATIONS

- USE EXAGGERATED EMOTIONS (SUPER SCARED, EXTREMELY HAPPY).
- ADD SOUND EFFECTS TO MATCH EMOTIONS.
- SWITCH VERY QUICKLY FOR EXTRA CHALLENGE.

CHARACTER WALKS

PLAYERS

6-20 PLAYERS

TIME

10 MINUTES

DESCRIPTION

PLAYERS EXPLORE HOW DIFFERENT CHARACTERS MOVE BY WALKING AROUND THE SPACE WITH VARIOUS TRAITS.

OBJECTIVE

TO EXPLORE BODY LANGUAGE AND CHARACTER CREATION.

INSTRUCTIONS

1. PLAYERS WALK AROUND THE SPACE.
2. THE FACILITATOR CALLS OUT A CHARACTER (A GIANT, A MOUSE, A SUPERHERO).
3. PLAYERS IMMEDIATELY CHANGE THEIR WALK TO FIT THE CHARACTER.
4. CONTINUE WITH DIFFERENT CHARACTERS.

VARIATIONS

- ADD EMOTIONS (SAD GIANT, HAPPY SUPERHERO).
- CHANGE TEMPO (SLOW MOTION, SUPER FAST).
- ASK PLAYERS TO INTERACT WITH EACH OTHER IN CHARACTER.

EMOTION ORCHESTRA

PLAYERS

8-20 PLAYERS

TIME

15 MINUTES

DESCRIPTION

THE GROUP BECOMES AN "ORCHESTRA" WHERE EACH PLAYER REPRESENTS AN EMOTION WITH SOUNDS AND GESTURES.

OBJECTIVE

TO EXPLORE EMOTIONS THROUGH SOUND AND MOVEMENT, AND PRACTICE GROUP COORDINATION.

INSTRUCTIONS

1. THE FACILITATOR IS THE CONDUCTOR.
2. EACH PLAYER IS ASSIGNED (OR CHOOSES) AN EMOTION.
3. WHEN THE CONDUCTOR POINTS TO THEM, THEY MAKE A SOUND/GESTURE FOR THAT EMOTION.
4. THE CONDUCTOR BUILDS A "SYMPHONY OF EMOTIONS" BY COMBINING PLAYERS.

VARIATIONS

- CHANGE VOLUME AND INTENSITY.
- SWITCH CONDUCTORS.
- BLEND EMOTIONS TOGETHER (HAPPY + SCARED).

WHO AM I?
(GUESSING CHARACTERS)

PLAYERS

6-15 PLAYERS

TIME

10 MINUTES

DESCRIPTION

A GUESSING GAME WHERE PLAYERS ACT LIKE A CHARACTER OR FAMOUS PERSON, AND THE GROUP MUST GUESS WHO IT IS.

OBJECTIVE

TO ENCOURAGE ACTING, CREATIVITY, AND OBSERVATION.

INSTRUCTIONS

1. ONE PLAYER SECRETLY RECEIVES OR THINKS OF A CHARACTER (TEACHER, PIRATE, SUPERHERO, FAMOUS SINGER).
2. THEY ACT IT OUT WITH MOVEMENTS, VOICES, OR BEHAVIORS.
3. THE REST OF THE GROUP GUESSES.
4. ROTATE UNTIL EVERYONE HAS PLAYED.

VARIATIONS

- ADD TIME LIMITS.
- PLAY IN TEAMS.
- USE ONLY MIME (NO SPEAKING).

CHARACTER INTERVIEWS

PLAYERS

4-12 PLAYERS

TIME

10-15 MINUTES

DESCRIPTION

ONE PLAYER TAKES ON A CHARACTER, AND OTHERS INTERVIEW THEM WITH QUESTIONS.

OBJECTIVE

TO PRACTICE IMPROVISING IN CHARACTER AND THINKING CREATIVELY.

INSTRUCTIONS

1. ONE PLAYER BECOMES A CHARACTER (PIRATE, TEACHER, ALIEN).
2. OTHER PLAYERS ASK THEM QUESTIONS.
3. THE CHARACTER MUST ANSWER IN ROLE.
4. SWITCH CHARACTERS SO MULTIPLE PLAYERS TRY.

VARIATIONS

- GIVE THE CHARACTER A SECRET (THEY'RE SCARED OF WATER, THEY LOVE CANDY).
- USE ONLY YES/NO QUESTIONS.
- INTERVIEW TWO CHARACTERS AT ONCE.

EMOTION SWITCH SCENES

PLAYERS

4-12 PLAYERS

TIME

10-15 MINUTES

DESCRIPTION

TWO PLAYERS PERFORM A SCENE, AND THE FACILITATOR CHANGES THE EMOTIONS DURING THE PERFORMANCE.

OBJECTIVE

TO PRACTICE ACTING FLEXIBILITY, LISTENING, AND EMOTIONAL RANGE.

INSTRUCTIONS

1. TWO PLAYERS BEGIN A SCENE (EXAMPLE: COOKING DINNER).
2. THE FACILITATOR CALLS OUT EMOTIONS (ANGRY, JOYFUL, NERVOUS).
3. THE PLAYERS MUST INSTANTLY SHIFT THEIR ACTING TO THAT EMOTION WHILE KEEPING THE SAME SCENE.
4. CONTINUE UNTIL THE SCENE REACHES AN ENDING.

VARIATIONS

- CHANGE EMOTIONS VERY RAPIDLY.
- ADD SOUND EFFECTS TO SUPPORT EMOTIONS.
- INVOLVE MORE PLAYERS IN THE SCENE.

CHARACTER SWAP

PLAYERS

4-12 PLAYERS

TIME

10-15 MINUTES

DESCRIPTION

TWO PLAYERS START A SCENE IN CHARACTER, THEN SWAP CHARACTERS WHEN THE FACILITATOR CALLS "SWITCH!"

OBJECTIVE

TO PRACTICE FLEXIBILITY, CHARACTER WORK, AND PLAYFUL IMPROVISATION.

INSTRUCTIONS

1. TWO PLAYERS START A SCENE (EXAMPLE: DETECTIVE AND THIEF).
2. AT ANY MOMENT, THE FACILITATOR CALLS "SWITCH!"
3. THE PLAYERS IMMEDIATELY SWAP ROLES AND CONTINUE THE SAME SCENE.
4. KEEP SWITCHING UNTIL THE SCENE ENDS.

VARIATIONS

- ADD MORE CHARACTERS AND SWITCH BETWEEN THREE OR FOUR.
- SWAP NOT ONLY ROLES BUT ALSO EMOTIONS.
- LET THE AUDIENCE CALL "SWITCH!"

OPPOSITES SCENE

PLAYERS

6-15 PLAYERS

TIME

10 MINUTES

DESCRIPTION

PLAYERS ACT OUT A SHORT SCENE, BUT THEY MUST ALWAYS DO OR SAY THE OPPOSITE OF WHAT MAKES SENSE.

OBJECTIVE

TO ENCOURAGE CREATIVITY, FLEXIBILITY, AND HUMOR.

INSTRUCTIONS

1. CHOOSE A SIMPLE SCENE (SHOPPING, CLASSROOM, RESTAURANT).
2. PLAYERS MUST RESPOND WITH THE OPPOSITE OF WHAT IS EXPECTED.
3. EXAMPLE: IF ASKED "ARE YOU HUNGRY?" THEY ANSWER, "NO, I'M ASLEEP!" AND PRETEND TO SNORE.
4. CONTINUE UNTIL THE SCENE ENDS OR BECOMES TOO SILLY.

VARIATIONS

- ADD "OPPOSITE EMOTIONS."
- SWITCH HALFWAY TO NORMAL ACTING.
- PLAY IN PAIRS OR LARGER GROUPS.

SUPERHERO ACADEMY

PLAYERS
6-20 PLAYERS

TIME
10-15 MINUTES

DESCRIPTION
PLAYERS INVENT SUPERHEROES WITH UNIQUE POWERS AND ATTEND A "TRAINING ACADEMY."

OBJECTIVE
TO EXPLORE IMAGINATION, CHARACTER BUILDING, AND TEAMWORK.

INSTRUCTIONS
1. EACH PLAYER CREATES A SUPERHERO WITH A NAME AND UNIQUE (FUNNY OR SERIOUS) POWER.
2. THE FACILITATOR IS THE "ACADEMY TEACHER" WHO GIVES MISSIONS OR TRAINING CHALLENGES.
3. PLAYERS SHOW HOW THEY USE THEIR POWERS IN EXERCISES (SAVING SOMEONE, FIGHTING VILLAINS).
4. THE GROUP CELEBRATES EACH SUPERHERO'S SUCCESS.

VARIATIONS
- PAIR SUPERHEROES INTO TEAMS.
- HAVE VILLAINS APPEAR.
- CREATE A "GRADUATION CEREMONY" FOR NEW HEROES.

PERFORMANCE & CONFIDENCE

PERFORMANCE & CONFIDENCE

Improvisation is about sharing stories bravely in front of others. These games help children build the confidence to perform — to step into the spotlight, take creative risks, and enjoy being seen and heard.

In this section, players practice how to:

- Perform with presence — standing tall, speaking clearly, and owning the stage.
- Work as an ensemble — supporting each other so everyone shines.
- Embrace mistakes — turning surprises into opportunities for laughter and learning.

These activities focus on stage awareness, self-expression, and trust. They prepare young improvisers for sharing their ideas not only in performance, but in everyday life — in class, in groups, or any time they need to speak up with confidence.

Use these games to:

- Transition from practice to performance.
- Help shy students find their voice.
- Strengthen group unity before a show or presentation.

Most of all, remind players that performing isn't about perfection — it's about connection, courage, and joy. When children feel safe and supported, they discover that the stage is not a place to fear... it's a place to shine.

ONE-MINUTE STORY

PLAYERS

3-12 PLAYERS

TIME

10-15 MINUTES

DESCRIPTION

EACH PLAYER TELLS AN IMPROVISED STORY THAT MUST LAST EXACTLY ONE MINUTE.

OBJECTIVE

TO PRACTICE STORYTELLING, TIMING, AND CONFIDENCE IN SPEAKING IN FRONT OF OTHERS.

INSTRUCTIONS

1. A PLAYER IS GIVEN A RANDOM THEME OR WORD.
2. THEY MUST TELL A STORY LASTING EXACTLY ONE MINUTE.
3. THE GROUP CHEERS THEM WHEN THEY FINISH.
4. ROTATE SO EVERYONE TRIES.

VARIATIONS

- TELL IT IN 30 SECONDS, THEN 10.
- TELL IT IN A DIFFERENT STYLE (NEWS, RAP, FAIRY TALE).
- SWITCH STORYTELLERS HALFWAY.

STATUE GALLERY

PLAYERS

6-20 PLAYERS

TIME

10-15 MINUTES

DESCRIPTION

PLAYERS POSE LIKE FROZEN STATUES WHILE THE REST OF THE GROUP WALKS AROUND AS IF IN A MUSEUM.

OBJECTIVE

TO PRACTICE STAGE PRESENCE, STILLNESS, AND COMFORT IN BEING OBSERVED.

INSTRUCTIONS

1. HALF THE PLAYERS BECOME STATUES AND FREEZE IN POSES.
2. THE OTHERS WALK AROUND OBSERVING THEM LIKE IN A MUSEUM.
3. AFTER A FEW MINUTES, SWITCH ROLES.

VARIATIONS

- ADD A THEME (UNDERWATER, SUPERHEROES, CIRCUS).
- VISITORS CAN INTERVIEW THE STATUES.
- STATUES COME ALIVE FOR 5 SECONDS.

'SHOWTIME!

PLAYERS

6-20 PLAYERS

TIME

15-20 MINUTES

DESCRIPTION

PLAYERS WORK IN SMALL GROUPS TO CREATE AND PERFORM A SHORT IMPROVISED "SHOW" USING SKILLS FROM PREVIOUS GAMES.

OBJECTIVE

TO CELEBRATE CREATIVITY, TEAMWORK, AND CONFIDENCE IN FRONT OF AN AUDIENCE.

INSTRUCTIONS

1. DIVIDE PLAYERS INTO SMALL GROUPS.
2. GIVE EACH GROUP A THEME, OBJECT, OR IDEA.
3. THEY HAVE 5 MINUTES TO PREPARE A SHORT SCENE.
4. EACH GROUP PERFORMS THEIR SHOW FOR THE OTHERS.

VARIATIONS

- ADD MUSIC OR SOUND EFFECTS.
- PERFORM IN DIFFERENT GENRES (COMEDY, MYSTERY, ACTION).
- MIX TWO RANDOM ELEMENTS (PIRATES + PIZZA).

'SPOTLIGHT MOMENTS

PLAYERS

6-20 PLAYERS

TIME

10-15 MINUTES

DESCRIPTION

EACH PLAYER TAKES A SHORT TURN IN THE "SPOTLIGHT" TO SHARE SOMETHING CREATIVE — A FUNNY WALK, A LINE OF DIALOGUE, A MADE-UP DANCE, OR EVEN A SOUND EFFECT. THE GOAL IS TO CELEBRATE BEING SEEN AND TO CHEER FOR OTHERS.

OBJECTIVE

TO BUILD STAGE CONFIDENCE, SELF-EXPRESSION, AND COMFORT PERFORMING IN FRONT OF OTHERS.

INSTRUCTIONS

1. CREATE A SMALL "STAGE AREA" IN THE CENTER OF THE ROOM — THE SPOTLIGHT ZONE.
2. ONE AT A TIME, PLAYERS STEP INTO THE SPOTLIGHT.
3. GIVE THEM 10-15 SECONDS TO PERFORM ANYTHING THEY WANT
4. AFTER EACH MINI-PERFORMANCE, THE GROUP CLAPS AND CHEERS LOUDLY!
5. CONTINUE UNTIL EVERYONE HAS HAD A TURN (OR TWO!).

VARIATIONS

- GIVE THE GROUP PROMPTS LIKE "SOMETHING MAGICAL," "SOMETHING NOISY," OR "SOMETHING FROM OUTER SPACE."
- LET TWO PLAYERS SHARE THE STAGE AT THE SAME TIME TO PERFORM TOGETHER.
- PERFORM ONLY USING MOVEMENT OR FACIAL EXPRESSION — NO WORDS ALLOWED!

TEAMWORK & COLLABORATION

TEAMWORK & COLLABORATION

Improvisation is a team sport! These games teach children how to work together, share ideas, and build stories as a group. In improvisation, there are no stars or solos — only partners who listen, support, and create together.

Through collaboration, players learn to:

- Say "yes, and..." — accepting and adding to others' ideas.
- Share focus — giving everyone a moment to shine.
- Build trust — knowing that the team has their back.

These activities remind children that the best scenes come from teamwork, not competition. Whether they're building a story, passing energy, or creating a scene together, they'll discover that creativity grows when everyone contributes.

Use these games to:

- Strengthen group connection and unity.
- Encourage empathy, patience, and respect.
- Help players support one another both on and off stage.

Encourage laughter, flexibility, and generosity — because when children learn to collaborate in play, they also learn to collaborate in life.
In improv, no one succeeds alone — every great moment is a shared creation.

PASS THE CLAP

PLAYERS

6-20 PLAYERS

TIME

15-20 MINUTES

DESCRIPTION

A CIRCLE GAME WHERE PLAYERS PASS A CLAP AROUND AS QUICKLY AND SMOOTHLY AS POSSIBLE.

OBJECTIVE

TO BUILD RHYTHM, FOCUS, AND GROUP CONNECTION.

INSTRUCTIONS

1. PLAYERS STAND IN A CIRCLE.
2. ONE PLAYER CLAPS WHILE FACING THE PERSON NEXT TO THEM.
3. THE NEXT PLAYER IMMEDIATELY CLAPS FACING THE NEXT PERSON, AND SO ON.
4. THE GOAL IS TO KEEP THE RHYTHM SMOOTH AND UNBROKEN.

VARIATIONS

- REVERSE DIRECTION AT ANY MOMENT.
- ADD A "DOUBLE CLAP" TO SKIP A PERSON.
- TRY TO GO FASTER AND FASTER.

YES, LET'S!

PLAYERS

6-20 PLAYERS

TIME

15-20 MINUTES

DESCRIPTION

PLAYERS ACCEPT EVERY IDEA BY RESPONDING WITH "YES, LET'S!" AND DOING IT TOGETHER.

OBJECTIVE

TO PRACTICE AGREEMENT, SPONTANEITY, AND GROUP ENERGY.

INSTRUCTIONS

1. PLAYERS STAND IN A CIRCLE.
2. ONE PLAYER SUGGESTS AN ACTION: "LET'S FLY LIKE BIRDS!"
3. EVERYONE ANSWERS: "YES, LET'S!" AND DOES THE ACTION TOGETHER.
4. ANOTHER PLAYER SUGGESTS SOMETHING NEW, AND REPEAT.

VARIATIONS

- DO IT WITH EMOTIONS ("LET'S CRY LIKE BABIES!").
- USE CHARACTERS ("LET'S BE ROBOTS!").
- PLAY IN SMALL GROUPS.

HUMAN KNOT

PLAYERS

8-15 PLAYERS

TIME

15-20 MINUTES

DESCRIPTION

PLAYERS FORM A "KNOT" BY HOLDING HANDS RANDOMLY AND MUST UNTANGLE THEMSELVES WITHOUT LETTING GO.

OBJECTIVE

TO BUILD COOPERATION, PATIENCE, AND PROBLEM-SOLVING.

INSTRUCTIONS

1. PLAYERS STAND IN A CIRCLE, SHOULDER TO SHOULDER.
2. EVERYONE PUTS THEIR HANDS IN THE CENTER AND GRABS TWO RANDOM HANDS.
3. WITHOUT LETTING GO, THE GROUP WORKS TO UNTANGLE INTO A CIRCLE AGAIN.

VARIATIONS

- TRY IT WITH EYES CLOSED.
- ADD A TIME LIMIT.
- PLAY IN SMALLER GROUPS FOR FASTER RESULTS.

GROUP MACHINE

PLAYERS

6-20 PLAYERS

TIME

10-15 MINUTES

DESCRIPTION

SIMILAR TO SHAPE MACHINES, BUT THIS TIME THE GROUP COLLABORATES TO BUILD ONE BIG MACHINE TOGETHER FROM THE START.

OBJECTIVE

TO PRACTICE SYNCHRONIZATION, CREATIVITY, AND TEAMWORK.

INSTRUCTIONS

1. PLAYERS START MOVING TOGETHER IN THE SPACE.
2. ONE PLAYER BEGINS A REPETITIVE MOVEMENT AND SOUND.
3. OTHERS JOIN IN, CONNECTING THEMSELVES PHYSICALLY OR RHYTHMICALLY.
4. THE WHOLE GROUP BECOMES ONE GIANT "MACHINE."

VARIATIONS

- ADD A THEME (FACTORY, TIME MACHINE, CIRCUS).
- SWITCH LEADERS TO CHANGE THE RHYTHM.
- END WITH THE MACHINE "BREAKING DOWN."

COLLABORATIVE DRAWING
(IN THE AIR OR ON PAPER)

PLAYERS

4-12 PLAYERS

TIME

10-15 MINUTES

DESCRIPTION

PLAYERS CREATE ONE DRAWING TOGETHER, EACH ADDING SMALL CONTRIBUTIONS IN TURN.

OBJECTIVE

TO FOSTER COOPERATION, IMAGINATION, AND COLLECTIVE CREATION.

INSTRUCTIONS

1. PLAYERS SIT OR STAND IN A CIRCLE.
2. ON A LARGE SHEET (OR IN THE AIR WITH GESTURES), ONE PLAYER STARTS DRAWING.
3. THE NEXT ADDS A DETAIL, THEN THE NEXT, AND SO ON.
4. THE RESULT IS A GROUP ARTWORK OR IMAGINARY "AIR DRAWING."

VARIATIONS

- GIVE A THEME (UNDERWATER WORLD, OUTER SPACE).
- DRAW SILENTLY WITHOUT SPEAKING.
- TURN THE DRAWING INTO A STORY.

SCENE WORK & GROUP GAMES

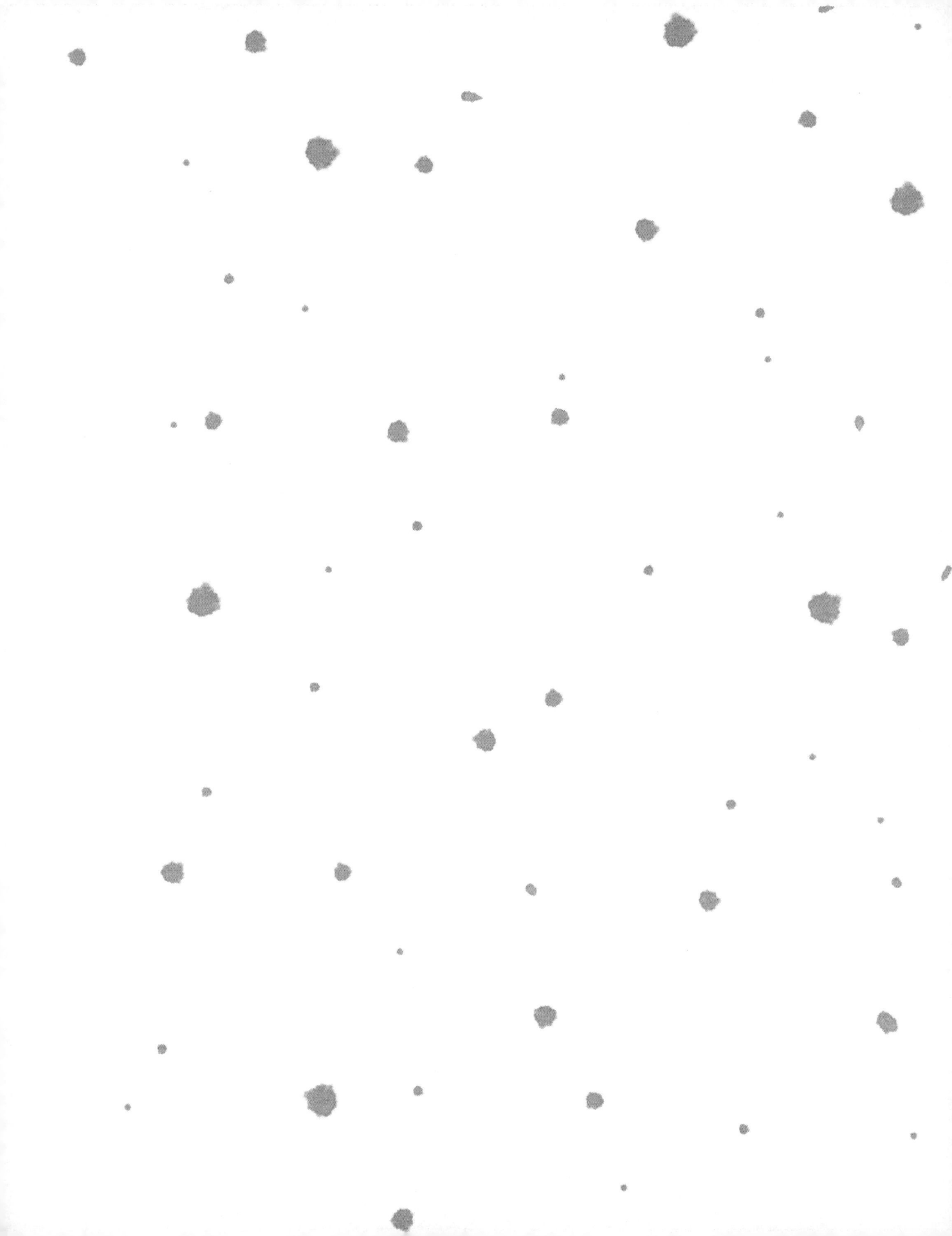

SCENE WORK & GROUP GAMES

Now it's time to bring everything together! In this section, players use their imagination, teamwork, and listening skills to create full improvised scenes and group performances.

These games help children understand how to:

- Build a scene from start to finish
- Collaborate as storytellers
- Stay present and react naturally

Scene work is where improvisation truly comes alive. Players become actors, directors, narrators, and audiences — all at once! They learn that stories don't need scripts when everyone listens, imagines, and plays with purpose.

Group games encourage unity and rhythm. They challenge children to think together, move together, and trust each other as a creative ensemble. The focus is always on teamwork, spontaneity, and having fun while building a story together.

Use these activities to:

- Transition from exercises to full improvisation scenes.
- Encourage collaboration and creative problem-solving.
- Build confidence in performing longer, more structured games.

'FREEZE TAG

PLAYERS

6-15 PLAYERS

TIME

10-15 MINUTES

DESCRIPTION

TWO PLAYERS IMPROVISE A SCENE. AT ANY MOMENT, ANOTHER PLAYER CAN YELL "FREEZE!", TAKE SOMEONE'S PLACE, AND START A NEW SCENE.

OBJECTIVE

TO ENCOURAGE CREATIVITY, SPONTANEITY, AND TEAMWORK.

INSTRUCTIONS

1. TWO PLAYERS START A SCENE.
2. AT ANY MOMENT, SOMEONE CAN SHOUT "FREEZE!"
3. THAT PERSON TAPS ONE PLAYER OUT, TAKES THEIR EXACT FROZEN POSITION, AND STARTS A NEW SCENE.
4. REPEAT UNTIL MANY PLAYERS HAVE PARTICIPATED.

VARIATIONS

- ONLY USE SPECIFIC THEMES (SPORTS, OUTER SPACE, FAIRY TALES).
- USE EXAGGERATED BODY POSITIONS.
- LIMIT SCENES TO 3 LINES EACH.

TWO-LINE SCENES

PLAYERS

4-12 PLAYERS

TIME

10 MINUTES

DESCRIPTION

PLAYERS PERFORM SHORT SCENES WHERE EACH PERSON CAN ONLY SAY ONE PRE-ASSIGNED LINE.

OBJECTIVE

TO PRACTICE CREATIVITY WITHIN RESTRICTIONS AND LEARN TO USE TONE AND EXPRESSION.

INSTRUCTIONS

1. EACH PLAYER IS GIVEN ONE LINE (E.G., "IT'S TOO LATE!" OR "I LOVE PIZZA.").
2. TWO PLAYERS CREATE A SCENE USING ONLY THEIR ASSIGNED LINES.
3. REPEAT WITH DIFFERENT PLAYERS AND LINES.

VARIATIONS

- USE SILLY OR DRAMATIC LINES.
- PLAYERS CAN CHANGE EMOTION WHILE SAYING THE SAME LINE.
- ADD A THIRD PLAYER WITH ANOTHER FIXED LINE.

THE BUS STOP

PLAYERS

4-12 PLAYERS

TIME

10-15 MINUTES

DESCRIPTION

A SIMPLE SCENE AT A BUS STOP WHERE CHARACTERS WITH DIFFERENT PERSONALITIES INTERACT.

OBJECTIVE

TO PRACTICE CHARACTER WORK, LISTENING, AND BUILDING SCENES TOGETHER.

INSTRUCTIONS

1. TWO PLAYERS SIT AT AN IMAGINARY BUS STOP.
2. A THIRD PLAYER ENTERS WITH A NEW PERSONALITY.
3. CHARACTERS INTERACT UNTIL ONE LEAVES.
4. KEEP ROTATING WITH NEW CHARACTERS.

VARIATIONS

- ADD EXAGGERATED QUIRKS (SINGS EVERYTHING, AFRAID OF BUSES).
- CHANGE THE LOCATION (AIRPORT, DENTIST, SPACESHIP).
- LET THE AUDIENCE SUGGEST QUIRKS.

PARTY QUIRKS

PLAYERS

6-12 PLAYERS

TIME

10-15 MINUTES

DESCRIPTION

ONE PLAYER HOSTS A PARTY, WHILE GUESTS COME IN WITH SECRET QUIRKS THE HOST MUST GUESS.

OBJECTIVE

TO PRACTICE CHARACTER ACTING, GUESSING, AND PLAYFUL INTERACTION.

INSTRUCTIONS

1. ONE PLAYER IS THE HOST.
2. THE OTHER PLAYERS EACH RECEIVE A SECRET QUIRK (E.G., THINKS THEY ARE A ROBOT, OBSESSED WITH BANANAS).
3. GUESTS ENTER ONE BY ONE AND ACT OUT THEIR QUIRK.
4. THE HOST INTERACTS AND TRIES TO GUESS EACH QUIRK.

VARIATIONS

- GUESTS CAN TEAM UP WITH QUIRKS THAT CONNECT.
- THE AUDIENCE CAN SUGGEST QUIRKS.
- ADD A TIME LIMIT FOR GUESSING.

CONDUCTED STORY

PLAYERS

6-20 PLAYERS

TIME

10-15 MINUTES

DESCRIPTION

PLAYERS TELL A STORY TOGETHER, BUT THE CONDUCTOR CHOOSES WHO SPEAKS BY POINTING AT THEM.

OBJECTIVE

TO PRACTICE TEAMWORK, LISTENING, AND STORY FLOW.

INSTRUCTIONS

1. ALL PLAYERS LINE UP.
2. THE FACILITATOR (CONDUCTOR) POINTS TO ONE PLAYER TO SPEAK.
3. AT ANY MOMENT, THE CONDUCTOR SWITCHES TO ANOTHER PLAYER.
4. TOGETHER THEY CREATE A CONTINUOUS STORY.

VARIATIONS

- ADD SOUND EFFECTS OR GESTURES.
- SWITCH VERY FAST FOR COMEDY.
- CHANGE GENRES MID-STORY (SCI-FI, WESTERN).

SOUND EFFECTS SCENE

PLAYERS

6-12 PLAYERS

TIME

10 MINUTES

DESCRIPTION

TWO PLAYERS ACT OUT A SCENE, WHILE OTHERS PROVIDE SOUND EFFECTS

OBJECTIVE

TO PRACTICE TEAMWORK, CREATIVITY, AND LISTENING.

INSTRUCTIONS

1. TWO PLAYERS BEGIN A SCENE (E.G., CAMPING, CAR RIDE).
2. OTHER PLAYERS MAKE SOUND EFFECTS (BIRDS, CARS, DOORS).
3. ACTORS MUST REACT NATURALLY TO THE SOUNDS.

VARIATIONS

- ADD WRONG OR SILLY SOUND EFFECTS.
- ROTATE ACTORS AND SOUND MAKERS.
- DO IT AS A SCARY OR ACTION SCENE.

DIRECTOR'S CUT

PLAYERS

6-15 PLAYERS

TIME

10-15 MINUTES

DESCRIPTION

PLAYERS PERFORM A SCENE WHILE A "DIRECTOR" INTERRUPTS, CHANGING STYLES, EMOTIONS, OR DETAILS.

OBJECTIVE

TO BUILD ADAPTABILITY, CREATIVITY, AND FUN GROUP PERFORMANCE.

INSTRUCTIONS

1. A GROUP OF PLAYERS STARTS A SCENE.
2. A "DIRECTOR" INTERRUPTS, CHANGING SOMETHING (GENRE: HORROR, MUSICAL, ACTION).
3. THE ACTORS INSTANTLY ADAPT AND CONTINUE.
4. THE DIRECTOR CAN KEEP INTERRUPTING WITH CHANGES.

VARIATIONS

- CHANGE LOCATION OR CHARACTERS MID-SCENE.
- ROTATE THE DIRECTOR ROLE.
- USE AUDIENCE SUGGESTIONS FOR CHANGES.

CLOSING GAMES
& REFLECTION

CLOSING GAMES & REFLECTION

Every good session deserves a meaningful ending. These closing games give children a chance to relax, celebrate, and reflect on what they've experienced together. After all the laughter, movement, and creativity, it's important to take a moment to slow down, breathe, and appreciate the journey.

In this section, players will:

- Reflect on what they learned, enjoyed, or discovered.
- Celebrate teamwork, courage, and creativity.
- Reconnect with calm energy before saying goodbye.

These activities help children recognize their own growth — not just as performers, but as kind, confident, and imaginative people. They remind the group that improv isn't about being perfect; it's about sharing joy and supporting one another.

Use these games to:

- End a workshop or class with a positive, grounded feeling.
- Strengthen the sense of community within the group.
- Encourage gratitude, empathy, and self-expression.

Encourage every child to take a moment of pride in what they've created — because in improv, every voice matters, every laugh counts, and every ending is a new beginning

COMPLIMENT CIRCLE

PLAYERS

6-20 PLAYERS

TIME

10 MINUTES

DESCRIPTION

PLAYERS SIT IN A CIRCLE AND TAKE TURNS GIVING EACH OTHER POSITIVE COMPLIMENTS.

OBJECTIVE

TO END THE SESSION WITH KINDNESS, CONNECTION, AND CONFIDENCE.

INSTRUCTIONS

1. PLAYERS SIT IN A CIRCLE.
2. ONE PLAYER GIVES A COMPLIMENT TO THE PERSON ON THEIR RIGHT.
3. CONTINUE AROUND THE CIRCLE UNTIL EVERYONE HAS RECEIVED A COMPLIMENT.

VARIATIONS

- COMPLIMENTS CAN BE ABOUT TODAY'S GAMES.
- COMPLIMENTS CAN BE NON-VERBAL (GESTURES, HIGH-FIVES).
- EACH PERSON GIVES ONE GROUP-WIDE COMPLIMENT.

'FREEZE & RELAX

PLAYERS
6-20 PLAYERS

TIME
10 MINUTES

DESCRIPTION
A CALMING GAME WHERE PLAYERS FREEZE ON COMMAND AND THEN RELAX SLOWLY.

OBJECTIVE
TO TRANSITION FROM HIGH ENERGY TO CALM FOCUS.

INSTRUCTIONS
1. PLAYERS MOVE AROUND THE SPACE FREELY.
2. THE FACILITATOR SAYS "FREEZE!" AND EVERYONE STOPS COMPLETELY.
3. THEN THE FACILITATOR SAYS "RELAX…" AND PLAYERS MELT SLOWLY TO THE GROUND OR INTO CALM STILLNESS.
4. REPEAT A FEW TIMES, ENDING WITH RELAXATION.

VARIATIONS
- ADD MUSIC FOR FREEZE/RELAX MOMENTS.
- TRY FUNNY FROZEN SHAPES BEFORE RELAXING.
- END WITH EVERYONE BREATHING TOGETHER.

ONE-WORD REFLECTION

PLAYERS

6-20 PLAYERS

TIME

5 MINUTES

DESCRIPTION

EACH PLAYER SHARES ONE WORD THAT DESCRIBES HOW THEY FEEL AT THE END OF THE SESSION.

OBJECTIVE

TO ENCOURAGE SELF-REFLECTION AND EMOTIONAL AWARENESS.

INSTRUCTIONS

1. PLAYERS STAND OR SIT IN A CIRCLE.
2. GOING AROUND, EACH SAYS ONE WORD ABOUT HOW THEY FEEL (E.G., "HAPPY," "TIRED," "EXCITED").
3. THE GROUP LISTENS RESPECTFULLY WITHOUT INTERRUPTIONS.

VARIATIONS

- PLAYERS CAN ALSO ADD A GESTURE TO MATCH THEIR WORD.
- WORDS CAN BE WRITTEN DOWN ON A BOARD OR PAPER.
- DO IT SILENTLY, JUST WITH GESTURES.

GROUP CELEBRATION DANCE

PLAYERS
6-20 PLAYERS

TIME
5 MINUTES

DESCRIPTION
THE WHOLE GROUP CELEBRATES TOGETHER WITH A BIG IMPROVISED DANCE TO END THE SESSION WITH JOY.

OBJECTIVE
TO FINISH WITH ENERGY, POSITIVITY, AND GROUP UNITY.

INSTRUCTIONS
1. PLAY UPBEAT MUSIC.
2. EVERYONE DANCES FREELY IN THE SPACE.
3. PLAYERS COPY EACH OTHER'S MOVES FOR FUN.
4. END WITH A BIG GROUP CHEER OR POSE.

VARIATIONS
- PASS THE "DANCE LEADER" AROUND THE CIRCLE.
- END WITH A FREEZE POSE.
- MAKE IT A SILENT DANCE WITH ONLY CLAPS AND STOMPS.

Printed in Dunstable, United Kingdom

71700846R00051